PRAISE FOR ELSP

In this compelling debut pamphlet]
an evocative collection that is raw,
intimate. The titles, themselves, aln. ──── poems in form,
take the reader on a journey through adolescence and beyond.
Key moments of life, both the poet's and the world beyond,
chronicled against modern culture, TV, songs, games, cinema...
Deeply evocative of a time and place in someone's life. We, the
reader, feel like we are there. Rustling sweet packets, eating Ben
and Jerry's, feeling the sun on our bare flesh. At times the honesty
holds the attention in a way that allows the reader to understand
a lived experience through the eyes and words of the poet — and
we are the wiser for the honour. These poems demand multiple
readings. Terrific.

Stephen Lightbown, Poet

Reflecting its own epigraph, Too Hot To Sleep is both 'too much,
and not enough'; too much in the way adolescence is —
overwhelming, stimulating, dragging the reader's attention
through the chaos of teen culture — and not enough, because it
would be impossible to have 'enough' of a collection so
compelling.

Elspeth manages to draw perfectly on the intensity of being a
teenager, turning the familiar lenses of pop culture back on the
reader, nurturing, excavating, and dragging parallels and mirrors
into life. The flood of images and references are powerful and
evocative, echoing teenage life perfectly.

She writes "it's easier / to forget about / flesh / if you're / rich."
and these poems are fleshy, centred in a changing body that
remains present throughout. This provides a counterweight to
the unreality of Sims and television characters, which function as

ciphers for a process of self-exploration, from family dynamics and teenage sexuality to sexual assault. Throughout, the climate crisis thrums under these evocative poems, grounding the writing with a sense of prescient foreboding.

Elspeth uses great precision, outlining heightened emotionality deftly, each reference well-balanced and expressive. Carefully crafted turns are unexpectedly slipped into poems, confronting the reader with their own intimate worlds "not knowing that aloneness is forced upon us", and the reminder that "there's so much worse / and so much better / to come".

Jamie Hale, Artistic Director, CRIPtic Arts

TOO
HOT
TO
SLEEP

Elspeth Wilson

About the author photo © Christy Ku @ christyku.co.uk

2nd Edition published 01/06/2023

ISBN: 978-1-9153202-7-8

Bent Key Publishing
Office 2, Unit 5
Palatine Industrial Estate
Causeway Avenue
Warrington
WA4 6QQ

bentkeypublishing.co.uk

Edited by Rebecca Kenny @ Bent Key
Cover art © Samantha Sanderson-Marshall @ SMASH Design and Illustration
smashdesigns.co.uk

Printed in the UK by Mixam Ltd.

To everyone who has been made to feel like they are too much,
and not enough

CONTENTS

Will I ever have as much fun again as I did at sleepovers aged fourteen 11

When *Teen Wolf* comes out I have not been sexually assaulted 12

The first time I hear *What Makes You Beautiful,* 13

I was watching my telescope when / Not only women get pregnant 15

Last birthday before thirteen 16

We all have side fringes in 2010 17

You are the golden 18

Picking your career aspiration is easier in Sims 2 than it is in Mrs Mackie's office where decades of work stare you down before you have even had your first orgasm 19

Flash floods kill six people the day Sabrina is remade 20

Option: 'Make Mess' or 'Cry Uncontrollably' 21

Sims as (every) bad day 22

Left-over musical differences 23

Wildfires burn across Australia as Edward Cullen takes his shirt off for the twentieth time 24

3AM Sims when it is too hot to sleep 26

Forever, with you 27

In Sims, I Woohoo with a girl 28

60% of bisexual people are in psychological distress at any one time 29

The Economy of Love 30

Sacrifice 31

Until We Didn't 32

Fountain 33

All the truths we've ever told 34

Pride 35

Acknowledgements / About the Author 37

About Bent Key 44

TOO
HOT
TO
SLEEP

WILL I EVER HAVE AS MUCH FUN AGAIN AS I DID AT SLEEPOVERS AGED FOURTEEN

We were up
all night
question
after
question
flooded
from my
lips, a tide
to stem
your yawns,
to sink your
tiredness
so the night
could stretch
on without
horizon (and
not just on repeat
in my mind).
Waves
of words
crashed
against my
teeth — I didn't
mind what the
answers
were, just
wanted to
keep you
talking

WHEN *TEEN WOLF* COMES OUT I HAVE NOT BEEN SEXUALLY ASSAULTED

Stiles, you were standing in the police station trying to solve a mystery like your life depended on it — and I suppose it did. You were wearing Straight Guy clothes, your hair grown out so you could get hotter in Season Two. So that there could be an extra heartthrob as your heart throbs so loud, surely Scott must hear it (when will you guys get together?). You speak in that generic American twang, your hands behind your head, blowing your newfound hair out your eyes. And then there is Scott — why, o why, can fan fiction not be real? Why can't we write into existence everything we want? Why can't 2012 go on forever and ever, bad jeans, worse hair, the taste of future on our tongues, baggy, oversized emotions that tear us apart with their claws, unknowing

there's   so much worse
              and so much better
              to come

THE FIRST TIME I HEAR *WHAT MAKES YOU BEAUTIFUL,*

I understand similes. I understand idioms. Those
ones that crawl out middle-aged mouths
cat paws that swipe
originality out the
door — tongues
sharpen them to the
point of
you
dancing
with golden spittle
spraying
from your
mouth, an open goalpost.
Your drunken pee
was music to my ears
as you dragged
me
from the kitchen dancefloor,
breaking the seal too early
breaking my heart too late.
I was in too deep as
you butchered Zayn,
murdered Harry
and forgot the names of the other three
knowing that you would be cute
no matter
what. Even at fifteen,
I knew that nothing could
ever sound as perfect
as your self-assured
pride as we screamed
ourselves

hoarse until there was nothing
left to speak
just our bodies bracketing
your teddy bear
as I listened to your
breath
and tried to slot
mine into your
rhythm

I WAS WATCHING MY TELESCOPE WHEN/NOT ONLY WOMEN GET PREGNANT

You're sired by Pollination Technician 135,
your pea-soup skin a reminder of
Good Vibes Only. Man
in the sky beamed me up
into that milky-way
smile all lime muscles and constellation
eyes, Here For a Good Time Not For A Long
Time tattooed on your plunging —
O! And it opened new vortexes,
galaxies I did not know existed,
temperatures yet to be discovered,
your flag posted in my
belly button. You showed
me the possibilities of my
body and then plonked me
down
to
earth

LAST BIRTHDAY BEFORE THIRTEEN

screams kept me awake
hot chocolate spills staining
chubby cloud smiles

decorating pens
drawing you on my pillow
so we always touch

newest girl at school
invited to sleepover
had to choose a bed

WE ALL HAVE SIDE FRINGES IN 2010

and we all have empty space beside our hearts
where our bras gape and tissues rustle.
Your arms

jiggle in the strip lights of your all-
white kitchen as we drag
each other upwards through air as Taylor tells us

Speak Now. My fingers dance with yours
in secret as beer is thrown over the lens that caught
us

that camera never worked again (sorry mum) but I didn't
need any external electricity to capture
the love-shaped red wine stains on your snake print jeans

YOU ARE THE GOLDEN

leaf in a sea of autumn
brown, your platinum
hair a spire in the smoky
haze of the B corridor
toilets as I skip across
puddles to you. Our eyes are
crimson, raw as my insides from our sleepover where I hogged the
mouse, confirmed every rumour about only
children — but it was just
because I wanted to create
a bigger family
together.

PICKING YOUR CAREER ASPIRATION IS EASIER IN SIMS 2 THAN IT IS IN MRS MACKIE'S OFFICE WHERE DECADES OF WORK STARE YOU DOWN BEFORE YOU HAVE EVEN HAD YOUR FIRST ORGASM

I am
raking it
in. It is
vulgar for
a poet to
think of metal
outside
metaphors
to see
(dollar)
signs not
similes. I
should
concern
myself
with art, not
affairs
of the flesh.
But in this
world — as
the Simoleons
stack up —
in this world,
it's easier
to forget
about
flesh
if you're
rich.

FLASH FLOODS KILL SIX PEOPLE THE DAY SABRINA IS REMADE

A lot has changed on set. My aunts' faces have shifted and Salem can move fluidly. Ambrose is better looking and Harvey is actually a teenager. There's a show in the neighbouring town with a high incidence of serial killers. But what I mostly notice is the seasons — the sun echoes my brittle blonde hair, a dry heat prickles damp necks that sweat like vegetables in plastic bags. No one mentions it on the Solstice when blood mixes with wine, a cocktail that goes straight to our feet, makes them dance with the devil (Dad crashes the party). No-one mentions it when my hair turns a whiter shade and everyone thinks I've dyed it, like it's not 104 degrees out there. No one mentions it. The wind ruffles through Greendale, a rasping cat's tongue. The heat must have turned up incrementally day by day, otherwise someone would have noticed it — because if they'd noticed it they'd have done something, right   right

OPTION: 'MAKE MESS' OR 'CRY UNCONTROLLABLY'

I self-generate the debris around me
after a failed birthday party. No
one wanted me to age up; dad was
too busy turning people into
vampires. Mum collapsed from
exhaustion. I make streamers from my
tears next to her prone body, a
cake's funeral next to my discarded
bassinet which had a use only half
an hour ago. Now
I can toddle and bawl and gurgle
and fart and ask for help all on my
own but do I really say *dag dag*
if no-one is listening?

SIMS AS (EVERY) BAD DAY

I am 15 days old. I am hungry and upset. I have been an adult for four days. Someone has removed the steps to my pool. They put them back when I start to wet myself, when I am forced to switch from breaststroke to doggy paddle. When I get out, the baby has stopped being a baby after three days. They grow up so fast that I don't have a toddler bed. And I do not have the ability to buy one.

LEFT-OVER MUSICAL DIFFERENCES

your hot pants were leather not denim
your hair was peroxide and sometimes
aquamarine caramel tones were only
for lattes you were a sophisticate
in Starbucks when I couldn't stand the taste of
you was more than I could bear you wore
red stilettos that weren't £8
from Next and you didn't fall
when you stomped in them your fur
jackets didn't swamp
you but for all your cool I could tell
there was a tiny heart beating
in the forest of hair
you knew all the lyrics but you didn't
sing them just wrote them on your bedroom
wall you were always going to be the one
who left I was just waiting to see what
trend you set as you
went

WILDFIRES BURN ACROSS AUSTRALIA AS EDWARD CULLEN TAKES HIS SHIRT OFF FOR THE TWENTIETH TIME

A thousand miles
away a country burns
as we decide it is time
for a Twilight
marathon
silvery moon
cold skin
in my heart
as Bella moves from Phoenix,
Arizona
making me see climate refugees
even in my YA
we cannot see the flames
like bees we are
asleep
smoked out
impervious
to our home
dissolving
Jacob says
to Edward
I'm hotter than you
which is true
but not all things that are true
are heard
new moon
breaking dawn
light still crawling
but as the sun cracks its yolk on
our popcorn husks
the dead
weight
in my stomach

is undying
I am cored
an apple
wishing
its pips will still be
seeded
find ground in which
to live
that the venomous bite
of rubbish
of sewage
of the crushed snail
of the dead wasp on the pavement
is not eternal
that the sharp pains in my chest will be
eclipsed
by action
(my own included)
and that it was okay
— forgive me —
to watch Bella and Edward
get their happy ending
whilst a country burned.

3AM SIMS WHEN IT IS TOO HOT TO SLEEP

We have two babies. Then three. Then four. Then we lose
count. There's no
stopping us. The sun shines, the snow falls, it's as
basic as that. Everything is how it's supposed
to be. There is no birth strike. There are no strikes
at all. Nothing will ever get hotter — except you
as you age — or colder than it should
be. There is a balance even my moods cannot
shake, nor the wind as it
ruffles the flowerbeds that are blooming
in March
in Scotland.

FOREVER, WITH YOU

Always is the word that teeters on Stefan's lips,
blossoming like a ripe fruit, a staple
crop to feed the masses.
Draped over his tongue, begging you to believe. But you can't
eat *always*. You can't
feed off empty promises,
good intentions that have you
hungry again in five minutes.
Immortality makes always a very long time,
just about as long as the nights that
kick into your abdomen. The
loss of him forced by the weakness of your own flesh.
Maybe he is not the love of your life
nor the love of your death.
Only time will tell — that is the one thing you don't have.
Patience is not a virtue in the
quiet evenings where your own mortal inadequacy
rallies around your heartbeat, a timer turned on one end.
Staring at the face that could solve your worries in
ten seconds, render your useless body
untouchable by anything other than werewolf
venom. Leave you with only skittering questions, like
what would it have been like to get a wrinkle?
X-ray vision won't deliver your answer. Take
yours with
zeal — darling, there is no sun setting at your back.

IN SIMS, I WOOHOO WITH A GIRL

The green diamond floats above
your head, your very own bar sign,
an invitation
to Express Affection and
Touch Fondly and maybe even
Express Undying
Love For on our second
date. You
bring the experience and I bring the
giant vibrating bed with the love-
heart and a fun rating of
ten. Your aspiration is to Woohoo
with fifteen sims and I am a
willing lump
under purple sheets.
Fireworks explode as my
hands touch the
mouse, click
again
    again
       again

60% OF BISEXUAL PEOPLE ARE IN PSYCHOLOGICAL DISTRESS AT ANY ONE TIME

The scalloped edge of the bra means the Roman sun burns my skin into a wave pattern. Once, we were on the beach we had made from the sandbox in your garden. Once, your boobs sat in this bra, not quite filling it, an electric gap between you and the lace. The lawn had been mowed, sweet smell escaping. We tried each other out for size, my pasty flesh spilling out of your bikini top as we sat in the mosaic sun of your patio. Your aunt inside the house, hoping its tidy perfection would rub off on her mind. Your father, trampling across the grass cuttings, leaving upon seeing the sight of us, declaring he didn't want a heart attack at forty. Free of those oppressive white walls, we laughed and laughed, our torsos shaped around each other like cuttings bent for a trellis. Now, my burn still aches with the touch of you, my skin less hot from the sun than when your fingers left their mark upon it.

THE ECONOMY OF LOVE

I believe that my body was born whole and fractured.

I believe that 2+2=4 and that people are not equations.

I believe that I can add you up and, still, you're a subtraction.

I believe that there is an x inside my head but it doesn't mark a spot and trigonometry won't help me solve it.

I believe that if numbers can turn from negative to positive then so can lives.

I believe that you can be one full circle and have complex segments.

I believe that the economy of love is faked and does not need to be rationed. Scarcity is a false principle. I will nationalise my heart and feed it to girls hungry for acceptance.

I believe that you are sorry.

I believe that for myself and not for you.

I believe that I can figure out my own rules and fill in my own blanks.

I believe that love plus love equals more than the sum of my parts.

SACRIFICE

The hope of your body that night stung my flesh, like a big toe sacrificed to test a hot bath. All the sunscreen my mother applied to my back that same morning could not protect me from the sizzle of our skin meeting in the dark, in the bed that was for a second a solar system — so large and yet so dense. Time bent along with our limbs, you making the first move as usual, me orbiting your sun, feeling warmth spread from my hacked-off pubes up past my nipples to where my hands lay like they were trying to hold in my womb. Like words would ruin this impossible, inevitable moment that couldn't be happening and was always going to happen. By the time you finished with me, my breath was clinging to my throat as tomato red clings to cheap Tupperware. A car horn was tooting and it was the same day mum had dropped me off and agreed to pick me up after dinner at eight. It was the same day but it was not the same day. Not at all.

UNTIL WE DIDN'T

We used to do Friday
cinema club until we
didn't. You used to
slide your damp hand
into mine, a fish into
a net as the credits
rolled. Your fingers
kept score on my
thigh tapping to
the latest action-
adventure. The red
velvet of the seats
was scrubbed bald
in the middle by other
backs, other shoulders,
where other heads
rested. Our breath
exhaled the same
as everyone else
in that room. We
used to think no-
one would pay any
attention to us

until they did.

FOUNTAIN

Dried chunks hacked off with blunt knives the morning after strawberries were forgotten in a sticky mess of boys boys boys girls girls girls and maybe something in between our teeth as we test each others' morning breath and it will always be like this, it will always be this flash that I remember, breaking off shards of dried up chocolate and eating them for breakfast, making something of the leftover sweetness

ALL THE TRUTHS WE'VE EVER TOLD

after Ace of Bass *by Fiona Benson*

That was the spring
we sat by the dappling lake
in a rationed heat, skin red where
we had been suntouched, white
bikini marks in places where the touches
were only ever our own
our chests mixed
with warm vodka
flat coke
ice turned slush puppy-eyed
pheromones as
the sun poked its
tongue through gap-teeth, lashed
our torsos
napped beneath those trees that smell like cum
fingered our nostril hairs, invited
our army of teeth to recite the folklore of that one time
saying it tasted like sex from fairytales
even though none of us knew that smell
— should not have known that smell —
just the sweeter salt
of our own fluids, finding out we liked our flavours, each other's
as we marched
time was sucked
up a plastic straw with cheap
nail varnish whisky,
hankering mouths chucked it back
spewed up all the truths we'd ever told
baby birds, our heads in the toilet,
not knowing this would never be regurgitated
for us
again.

PRIDE

The rustling of sweet packets and the green fire exit sign threaten to upset the delicate balance in my brain but that cinema smell of leather seats tells me to keep going. It says you don't know what you might find, you don't yet know all the things you are made of, all the pretty colours of dreams and fights and laughter and breakups and orgasms and hangovers and protests and tears and parties. Not just pinks and blues. Hope is on the big screen as I bite into my Ben and Jerry's Cookie Dough, not knowing my life will be changed in the next one hundred and twenty minutes. Not knowing that aloneness is forced upon us, a carving knife between the ribs. Not knowing that the first step against their tactics is to reach across the soft fabric of the seats and clasp her hand. The first time is in darkness but the next will be in light.

ACKNOWLEDGEMENTS

There are so many people who contributed to this work coming into the world, and without whose support my life and creative practice would be so much less rich, enjoyable and meaningful. To all of you, I'm forever grateful and hope you know how much you mean to me.

My first thanks go to Bec and the rest of the team at Bent Key Publishing for their transparency, ethics and commitment to the writing community, and for seeing the potential in my work. I'm honoured to be part of such a caring and passionate group of writers.

Thank you also to all the magazines and organisations that published versions of these poems — Vaine magazine, the Young Poets Network and the Moth, I'm very grateful that you supported my work as I developed as a poet.

This pamphlet would not exist in this form without Rachel Lewis, an excellent poet and thinker and writing BFF extraordinaire. You supported this pamphlet from the start and made me believe in its importance. You also gave me honest, useful feedback which helped make the manuscript shine and sing as much as possible.

And to Aoife, I really would never have started writing without you. You have a gorgeous, kind way of looking at and writing about the world, and I miss the days when we lived so close to each other and were able to share our writing all the time. I'm so grateful to have you in my life.

The writing community in general has been incredibly important to me, during both highs and lows, and there's so many people who have cheered me up, cheered me on and who

I'm grateful to have learned so much from. I'm thinking of Nadia, Christy, Kath, Anna, PM, Lucy, Elizabeth, Kerry, Polly — thank you for sharing your thoughts and your voices, and being your beautiful selves. You're like little bright points of light in a sometimes confusing, frustrating (literary) world.

To my writing mentors, Stephen Lightbown and Jamie Hale, my thanks for supporting me right from the start as a new poet and fostering my curiosity and my voice. You were always encouraging, patient and so generous with your time, and I'm honoured you chose to bestow all those gifts on me. The same can be said of my wonderful agent, Caro, who supports every writing endeavour I do, regardless of whether it is part of their official role or not!

To all my friends outside the writing community, thank you for being so supportive in my (sometimes rocky) writing journey. Katherine, you showed me what living a creative life could look like from when we were only teenagers, and you've always been so brave and persistent. I am in awe of your talent but more importantly your resilience and openness to learning and trying new things – thank you for always being there for me to have a moan when I haven't been paid on time (again).

Lisa, you are my greatest cheerleader and your generosity of spirit has kept me going through the toughest times – our teenage escapades with Laura and Elishka form so much of the backdrop of this collection, and I can't think of a better group of people to get into so many scrapes with.

Gregory Puffin, you have been the person I have shared my writing with when I was too embarrassed to share with anyone else, and you have also been a beautiful muse — I adore writing poems about our time together.

Bea, the immense love and support you've shown me since we met has been so instrumental in who I've become. The fact you took my writing seriously helped me take it seriously, too, and you are forever such a beacon of fun and joy in my life.

Daisy, your beautiful, sensitive way of looking at the world has taught me so much and I hope you know that my life was changed so much for the better on the day I met you. Thank you for accompanying to my readings in the face of cold weather and uncomfy seats.

I am blessed that there are too many friends for me to thank here but I hope you know who you are and how much I love you.

And to my mum and dad without whom none of this would have been possible (literally!). Growing up, you gave me the tools, confidence and love to have fun, play and experiment and I hope you know that everything I do is really a testament to that and to you.

Lastly, thank you, D. I genuinely wouldn't be who I am or know myself so well without you. Sometimes, my writing demands a lot of me, and you endlessly provide feedback, tech support, affection and patience. I couldn't think of a better person to spend this creative, messy life with.

ABOUT THE AUTHOR

Photo : Christy Ku

Elspeth Wilson is a Scottish writer and poet. Her hybrid prose-poetry work has been shortlisted for the Canongate Nan Shepherd Prize and Penguin's *Write Now* editorial programme. When she's not writing, she can usually be found in or near the sea.

ABOUT BENT KEY

It started with a key.

Bent Key is named after the bent front-door key that Rebecca Kenny found in her pocket after arriving home from hospital following her car crash. It is a symbol of change, new starts, risk and taking a chance on the unknown.

Bent Key is a micropublisher with ethics. We do not charge for submissions, we do not charge to publish and we make space for writers who may struggle to access traditional publishing houses, specifically writers who are neuro-divergent or otherwise marginalised. We never ask anyone to write for free, and we like to champion authentic voices.

All of our beautiful covers are designed by our graphic designer Sam at SMASH Design & Illustration, a graphic design company based in Southport, Merseyside.

Find us online:
bentkeypublishing.co.uk

Instagram & Facebook   @bentkeypublishing
Twitter   @bentkeypublish